cookies

NEW
HOLLAND

Published in 2013 by

New Holland Publishers

London • Sydney • Cape Town • Auckland

www.newhollandpublishers.com

Garfield House 86–88 Edgware Road London W2 2EA United Kingdom

1/66 Gibbes Street Chatswood NSW 2067 Australia

Wembley Square First Floor Solan Road Gardens Cape Town 8001 South Africa

218 Lake Road Northcote Auckland New Zealand

A catalogue record of this book is available at the British Library and the National Library of Australia.

ISBN: 9781742573793

Publisher: Fiona Schultz

Design: Keisha Galbraith

Production director: Olga Dementiev

Printer: Toppan Leefung Printing Limited (China)

10 9 8 7 6 5 4 3 2 1

Endpapers: Istock image

Follow New Holland Publishers on

Facebook: www.facebook.com/NewHollandPublishers

contents

Introduction

Nothing beats the smell and taste of freshly baked cookies. Often recalling fond memories of childhood afternoons spent watching the clock, waiting for those delicious treats to emerge, cookies hot from the oven are always welcome.

And even though everyone has their own personal favourite – whether it's a simple biscotti, a classic chocolate chip, or something more elaborate – you're sure to find in this book a recipe to please any palate, simple or sophisticated, young or old. We have brought together our most requested recipes in this exciting collection of cookies, and we know you'll enjoy hours of successful baking followed by hours of satisfying eating.

The basics

When making any recipe for the first time, take a little extra time to read it from beginning to end. Although a lot of the recipes in this book use similar methods, there may be subtle differences. Next, check through the ingredients and make sure you have enough of each. There's nothing worse than starting a recipe only to find you have to go down the street for more sugar!

Allow farm ingredients stored in the refrigerator, such as butter and eggs, to come to room temperature before using – cold ingredients can cause the mix to contract and become tough.

Many people prefer the rich flavour and moist texture that full-cream milk gives to their cooking, although the more health-conscious will prefer to use skimmed or low-fat milk. Either way, once again the milk should be at room temperature. A useful technique is to measure out the required amount of milk, cover it with cling wrap so it can come to room temperature, then return the carton or bottle to the refrigerator to keep it fresh.

Sift the dry ingredients together and make sure they are mixed through thoroughly. Lumps in the flour in the early stages can cause hard, white lumps to end up in the final mix, which is not a desirable outcome.

Baking powder, if poorly mixed through, can react with the skin of fruits and nuts such as raspberries, blueberries and walnuts, causing natural dyes to leach out of the ingredients – resulting in odd coloured stains. Although perfectly harmless, these stains indicate that perhaps a little more care and gentle handling is needed during the preparation stage!

To get the premium flavour from nuts, ensure they're fresh and give them a gentle toasting in a warm oven for a few minutes to bring out their flavours. Evenly spread the nuts over an ovenproof tray covered with baking paper. Toast almonds and hazelnuts at 350°F (180°C) for 10 minutes, walnuts and pecans should be toasted a little more gently at 325°F (160°C) for 10 minutes, and macadamias at 300°F (150°C) for the same period. Keep an eye on the nuts as you toast them, too, as they can change colour and burn very rapidly if left unattended. They should develop a lovely golden hue, but nothing darker. This technique for toasting nuts may also be used for other dishes, savoury or sweet, where you need a little extra flavour from them.

Remember not to overload the cookies with extra fillings – sometimes it can be too much of a good thing! Fold in ingredients such as chocolate and nuts after the dough is made, to help distribute them evenly. If you add the fillings to the dry ingredients, the flour will stick to the nuts or chocolate, stopping them from becoming part of the dough.

To make cleaning a lot easier, a little bit of cooking oil can be used to coat utensils before use. If using honey, maple syrup, golden syrup or treacle, a little oil brushed on the cup or measuring spoon will stop the sticky liquid from adhering, making for a more accurate measure and less time at the sink.

Chocolate can be melted in a ceramic cup in the microwave, but the traditional method is still the best. Break the chocolate up into small pieces and put it in a heatproof bowl sitting on top of a saucepan containing barely simmering hot water (a double boiler). Stir the chocolate as it melts and never let water get into the chocolate, as this will cause it to become granular. If you do end up with water in your chocolate, add a dash of cooking oil to help it return to the desired texture.

Equipment

A small selection of mixing bowls, wooden spoons and whisks should suffice for the preparation of basic cookie dough, although if you have an electric mixer and a few spatulas, you will definitely find them useful.

Quality scales and measuring cups are a major help. Make sure you choose measuring cups where the metric cup measures 9 fl oz (250ml). Small, nested sets of measuring cups are also useful, as are tablespoon and teaspoon measures. If investing in baking equipment, for absolute ease of measuring purchase scales that can measure liquid as well as dry ingredients.

It is also a good idea to make sure that your oven heats accurately. To check, purchase an oven thermometer and heat your oven to 400°F (200°C). Place the oven thermometer inside and leave it for 30 minutes. Remove the thermometer and check that it registers within 40°F (5°C). If not, it may be time to call a technician to re-adjust the oven temperature.

Ingredients

Quality ingredients are always important. Make sure your flour is fresh, especially if using wholemeal or rye flour. To check, stir a spoonful or two into a glass of warm water. The aroma should be pleasantly floury, not bitter or sour.

Purchase good quality cocoa and chocolate, and store nuts in airtight containers away from the light, or in the freezer so they remain at their best for as long as possible. Buy coconut as necessary and make sure that cream, buttermilk and all other dairy products are fresh.

When using fresh fruit in recipes, ensure they are firm or soft, as the recipe dictates. For example, using a firm banana where a soft one is called for will change the essence of the recipe. And where possible, always buy what's in season and not just what is in the supermarket – this way you will get well-priced, quality ingredients every time.

Types of cookies

The following is a list of some of the most common types of cookie:

- Twice baked cookies – the original cookie – are as popular as ever, especially in their native Europe. First, the dough is poured onto a tray, cooked, then cut to the desired thickness. The cookies are then baked again, which removes most of the moisture and makes them crisp.
- Drop cookies are very common and consist of a relatively soft dough placed or dropped onto the baking tray. As they cook, they spread and flatten. The classic chocolate chip cookie is often made using this method.
- Moulded cookies use a stiffer dough than drop cookies so they can be moulded into different shapes before cooking.
- Rolled cookies also use a relatively stiff dough that can be rolled flat then cut into the desired shape using a cookie cutter – gingerbread men are typical rolled cookies.
- Refrigerator cookies are similar to rolled cookies – they consist of a stiff dough that is refrigerated to become even stiffer. The dough is then shaped, often into a cylinder, and sliced to create a round cookie. Of course, other shapes are also possible.
- Sandwich cookies are exactly what their name suggests – two cookies sandwiching a filling, usually icing, although many other fillings are also suitable.

The key to good cookies

- Try to ensure you accurately follow the recipe – even a small deviation can have unexpected results.
- Be gentle with your cookies – they are often still quite soft when they emerge from the oven.
- Store your cookies in an airtight container, as they will go soft if they become stale.

classics

Traditional Shortbread

preparation 10 mins   **cooking** 30 mins
makes 25

9oz (250g) butter, at room
   temperature

1 cup confectioners' (icing)
   sugar

1 cup cornstarch (cornflour)

1 cup all-purpose (plain) flour

Preheat oven to 300°F (150°C). Lightly butter a baking tray.

Cream butter and confectioners' sugar until light and fluffy. Sift cornstarch and flour together. Mix sifted ingredients into creamed mixture, and knead well.

Roll out between two sheets of baking paper to ½in (1cm) thickness. Cut into 1¼ x 2¾in (3 x 7cm) fingers, then place on the baking tray. **Prick** around the edges with a fork.

Bake for 30 minutes or until pale golden.

Coconut Macaroons

preparation 10 mins   **cooking** 15 mins
makes 20

1⅓ cups desiccated coconut

⅓ cup sugar

2 tablespoons all-purpose (plain)
  flour

⅛ teaspoon salt

2 egg whites, whisked

½ teaspoon almond extract

Preheat oven to 325°F (160°C). Lightly butter a
baking sheet.

Combine coconut, sugar, flour and salt in a bowl.
Stir in egg whites and almond extract. Mix well.

Drop teaspoonfuls onto the baking sheet. Bake
for 15 minutes or until edges are brown. Remove
from sheets at once.

Brandy Snaps

preparation 20 mins **cooking** 8 mins
makes 30

4oz (125g) butter, at room
   temperature

⅔ cup sugar

¼ cup golden syrup

1 cup all-purpose (plain) flour

1 teaspoon ground ginger

Preheat oven to 350°F (180°C). Lightly butter 4 baking trays.

Cream butter and sugar. Add golden syrup, sift in flour and ginger, then mix.

Drop tablespoons of mixture onto the baking trays, no more than 4 or 5 to a tray. Allow room for spreading.

Bake for about 8 minutes or until golden. Cool slightly until able to be removed without collapsing. Slide brandy snaps from tray and cool on a rack until set.

Monte Carlos

preparation 15 mins **cooking** 12 mins
makes 20

9oz (250g) butter, at room
temperature

1 cup brown sugar

3 teaspoons vanilla extract

1 egg, lightly beaten

1 cup all purpose (plain) flour,
sifted

¼ cup self-rising (self-raising)
flour, sifted

1 cup desiccated coconut

¾ cup rolled oats

1 cup confectioners' (icing) sugar

½ cup raspberry jam

Preheat oven to 350°F (180°C). Lightly butter a
baking tray.

Place half the butter, the brown sugar and
2 teaspoons of the vanilla in a bowl and beat until
light and fluffy. Add the egg, all-purpose flour, self-
rising flour, coconut and rolled oats, and mix well
to combine.

Roll heaped tablespoonfuls of the mixture into
oval balls, place on the baking tray and flatten
slightly with a fork. Bake for 12 minutes or until
golden. Transfer to a wire rack to cool.

Place the remaining butter, the confectioners'
sugar and remaining vanilla in a bowl and beat
until light and fluffy.

Spread half the biscuits with raspberry jam and
top with the confectioners' sugar mixture. Top
with the remaining biscuits.

Florentines

preparation 25 mins   **cooking** 10 mins
makes 20

4oz (125g) butter, at room
   temperature

½ cup sugar

5 tablespoons golden syrup

¼ cup all-purpose (plain) flour

1 cup sliced almonds

½ cup glacé cherries, chopped

½ cup walnuts, chopped

¼ cup mixed peel, chopped

5oz (150g) cooking chocolate

Preheat oven to 350°F (180°C). Line 4 oven trays
with baking paper.

Cream butter and sugar, then beat in golden
syrup. Sift in flour, add almonds, cherries, walnuts
and peel and mix well.

Place tablespoonfuls of mixture onto a tray,
leaving plenty of room for the cookies to spread.
Using a knife, press each one out as flat and
round as possible. Cook no more than 4 or 5 to
a tray.

Bake for 10 minutes or until golden brown.
Remove from oven and leave on tray for
5 minutes before transferring to a wire rack.

Meanwhile, melt chocolate in a bowl over
simmering water. When the biscuits are cold, ice
with chocolate on their flat sides.

Melting Moments

preparation 20 mins   **cooking** 20 mins
makes 16

7oz (200g) butter, at room
  temperature

¾ cup confectioners' (icing) sugar

1 cup all-purpose (plain) flour

1 cup cornstarch (cornflour)

½ teaspoon baking powder

¼ cup raspberry jam

Preheat oven to 350°F (180°C). Lightly butter an oven tray.

Cream butter and confectioners' sugar until light and fluffy. Sift flour, cornstarch and baking powder together. Add to butter mixture and mix well.

Roll dough into balls the size of large marbles and place on the oven tray. Flatten slightly with a floured fork. Bake for 20 minutes or until cooked.

Allow to cool completely, then sandwich two biscuits together with raspberry jam. Repeat with remaining biscuits.

Iced VoVos

preparation 35 mins **cooking** 10 mins
makes 24

2oz (60g) butter, at room
temperature

½ cup superfine (caster) sugar

1 egg

⅔ cup all-purpose (plain) flour,
sifted

⅔ cup self-rising (self-raising)
flour, sifted

½ cup superfine (caster) sugar

¾ tablespoon gelatine powder

1 teaspoon vanilla extract

½ cup desiccated coconut

⅓ cup raspberry jam

Preheat oven to 350°F (180°C). Line 2 oven trays
with baking paper.

Beat the butter and sugar until light and creamy.
Add the egg, beat until combined, and fold in flours.

Turn dough onto floured surface and knead gently
for 1 minute or until smooth. Roll out between two
sheets of baking paper until ¼in (4mm) thick. Cut
into 2 x 2¼in (5 x 6cm) rectangles and place on
oven trays 1in (3cm) apart.

Bake for 10 minutes or until lightly golden. Cool
on the trays.

Meanwhile, combine superfine sugar and ⅓ cup
water in a small saucepan, then sprinkle in gelatine powder. Stir over low heat until dissolved.
Bring to the boil, then reduce heat and simmer for
4–5 minutes. Remove and cool.

When almost cold, pour into a bowl, add vanilla
and beat with an electric mixer for 3–4 minutes
until a very thick marshmallow forms. Spoon into
a piping bag fitted with a plain 1cm nozzle. Pipe
along each side of the biscuit, leaving a bare strip
in the middle. Dip the marshmallow in the coconut
and shake off the excess.

Put the jam in a small pan and heat gently until
thinned and warm. Spread down the centre of
each biscuit. Sprinkle with a little more coconut.

Gingerbread Men

preparation 20 mins   **cooking** 10 mins
makes 12

4oz (125g) butter, at room
  temperature

½ cup brown sugar, firmly packed

1 egg yolk

2½ cups all-purpose (plain) flour

1 teaspoon baking soda
  (bicarbonate soda)

3 teaspoons ground ginger

½ cup golden syrup

Preheat oven to 350°F (180°C). Line an oven tray
with baking paper.

Beat the butter and sugar together until light
and Sift dry ingredients together, then stir into
butter mixture with the golden syrup. Mix to a
light dough and knead gently on a lightly floured
surface until smooth.

Roll out between 2 sheets of baking paper
until approximately ¼in (3mm) thick. Using a
gingerbread man cookie cutter, cut gingerbread
men from the dough (re-roll the leftover dough
to make more gingerbread men), place on the
oven tray and bake for 10 minutes or until lightly
golden. Cool on the tray.

Yoyos

preparation 20 mins   **cooking** 20 mins
makes 10

6oz (175g) butter, at room
   temperature, plus 1¾oz (50g)

¼ cup confectioners' (icing) sugar,
   plus ½ cup

½ teaspoon vanilla extract

1⅓ cups all-purpose (plain) flour

¼ cup custard powder, plus
   2 tablespoons

Preheat oven to 350°F (180°C). Lightly butter an
oven tray.

Cream 6oz (175g) butter and ¼ cup confectioners'
sugar until light and fluffy, then add vanilla. Sift flour
and ¼ cup custard powder together. Mix sifted
ingredients into creamed mixture.

Roll tablespoonfuls of mixture into balls. Place on
oven tray and flatten with a fork. Bake for 15–20
minutes.

Meanwhile, beat remaining 1¾oz (50g) butter,
confectioners' sugar and custard powder
together until well combined.

When the biscuits have cooled completely,
sandwich two biscuits together with butter
and confectioners' sugar mixture. Repeat with
remaining biscuits.

citrus

Ginger Lemon Drops

preparation 10 mins **cooking** 20 mins
makes 20

½ cup all-purpose (plain) flour

⅓ cup superfine (caster) sugar

¼ teaspoon baking soda
   (bicarbonate soda)

pinch of salt

2 tablespoons ground ginger

¼ teaspoon ground cinnamon

½ teaspoon lemon essence

2oz (55g) unsalted butter

1 tablespoon golden syrup

1 small egg

Preheat oven to 350°F (180°C). Lightly butter a baking tray.

Sift flour, sugar, baking soda and salt into a bowl. Add ginger, cinnamon and lemon essence. Work in butter with hands until the mixture resembles breadcrumbs.

Beat golden syrup and egg together and gradually add to flour mix to form a dough.

Form into small balls and place well apart on the baking tray. Bake for 15–20 minutes until crisply golden.

Lemon Jumbles

preparation 20 mins **cooking** 15 mins
makes 12

1½oz (45g) butter, at room
temperature

¼ cup superfine (caster) sugar

½ egg

½ teaspoon lemon essence

½ cup all-purpose (plain) flour,
sifted

½ cup self-rising (self-raising)
flour, sifted

1 tablespoon milk

Preheat oven to 325°F (160°C).

Cream butter and sugar in an electric mixer. Mix
in egg and lemon essence, then add the flours
and mix to a firm dough.

On a floured surface, roll the dough out until
about ¼in (5mm) thick. Cut into lots of different
shapes and glaze with milk.

Bake for 10–15 minutes

Sweet Orange Hearts

preparation 20 mins   **cooking** 12 mins
makes 20

3oz (90g) all-purpose (plain) flour

1oz (30g) cornstarch (cornflour)

1½oz (45g) butter

1½oz (45g) sugar

2 eggs, lightly beaten

3 drops orange essence

zest of 1 orange

pink sprinkles to decorate

BUTTER CREAM FILLING
1¾oz (50g) butter,
   at room temperature

2 tablespoons milk

2 cups confectioners' (icing) sugar

3 drops pink food colouring

GLACÉ FROSTING
1½ cups confectioners' (icing)
   sugar

1 drop pink food colouring

3 tablespoons orange juice

Preheat oven to 350°F (180°C). Line an oven tray with baking paper.

Sift flour with cornstarch, then rub in the butter with your fingers. Add sugar, then eggs, orange essence and zest, stir to a stiff consistency.

Roll out thinly and cut with a heart-shaped cookie cutter. Place on baking paper and bake for 10–12 minutes.

Meanwhile prepare the butter cream filling. Beat the butter for 1 minute. Add milk and half the confectioners' sugar and beat for 2 minutes. Add remaining confectioners' sugar and the food colouring and beat until mixture is light and fluffy, about 5 minutes.

Combine thoroughly all glacé frosting ingredients in a separate small bowl.

Remove biscuits from oven, place on a wire rack until cold, then sandwich two biscuits together with butter cream filling. Top with glacé frosting and sprinkles, then repeat with remaining biscuits.

Citrus Snaps

preparation 50 mins **cooking** 12 mins
makes 45

6½oz (185g) butter, at room
  temperature

1 cup superfine (caster) sugar

1 teaspoon lemon essence

2½ cups all-purpose (plain) flour

1 egg, plus 1 yolk

zest of 1 lemon

zest of 1 lime

Preheat oven to 350°F (180°C). Line 2 baking trays with non-stick baking paper.

Place the butter, sugar and lemon essence in a food processor and process until smooth. Add the flour, egg, egg yolk and zests and process until a smooth dough forms. Knead the dough lightly, wrap in cling wrap and refrigerate for 30 minutes.

Roll out the dough between two sheets of non-stick baking paper until ¼in (5mm) thick. Cut the dough into circles using a 2in (5cm) round cookie cutter and place on baking trays.

Bake for 10–12 minutes or until golden. Cool on wire racks.

Lemon Short Stars

preparation 20 mins **cooking** 15 mins
makes 35

4oz (125g) all-purpose (plain) flour

4oz (125g) rice flour

4oz (125g) superfine (caster) sugar

4oz (125g) butter

1 egg yolk

2 tablespoons single (thickened) cream

1 cup confectioners' (icing) sugar

⅓ cup lemon juice

zest of 1 lemon

Preheat oven to 375°F (190°C). Line 2 oven trays with baking paper.

Mix flours and superfine sugar, then rub in the butter until the mixture resembles breadcrumbs. Beat the egg yolk, add to the flour mixture with the cream and mix to make a very stiff paste.

Roll out to an even thickness and cut out cookies with a star-shaped cutter. Place on a baking tray and bake for about 15 minutes, until a pale golden brown.

Meanwhile combine the confectioners' sugar, lemon juice and zest.

Remove biscuits from the oven and cool on a wire rack. Decorate with the lemon icing.

Lime, Clove and Nut Cookies

preparation 20 mins **cooking** 20 mins
makes 20

9oz (250g) unsalted butter, at
room temperature

2½oz (80g) confectioners' (icing)
sugar

¼ teaspoon lime essence

zest of 2 limes

½ teaspoon ground cloves

5oz (150g) all-purpose (plain)
flour

4½oz (130g) cornstarch
(cornflour)

½ teaspoon baking powder

5oz (150g) Brazil or macadamia
nuts, roughly chopped

Preheat oven to 340°F (170°C). Line 2 baking
trays with baking paper.

Cream butter, confectioners' sugar, lime
essence, zest and cloves until creamy and very
well combined. Sift flours and baking powder into
the butter mixture, mix well, then fold in the nuts.

Roll mixture into balls, 1 heaped tablespoonful
at a time, then place them on the baking trays,
leaving at least 2in (5cm) between each.

Flatten slightly and bake for 15–20 minutes,
until they just begin to turn golden. Cool on the
trays for 5 minutes, then transfer to a rack to cool
completely.

Lemon Yoghurt Cookies

preparation 15 mins, plus 12 hrs refrigeration **cooking** 20 mins
makes 12

1¾oz (50g) butter

2oz (60g) superfine (caster) sugar

1¾oz (50g) almond meal

3½oz (100g) all-purpose (plain) flour

zest of 1 lemon

4 tablespoons Greek-style yoghurt

¼ cup confectioners' (icing) sugar

2 drops lemon essence

Melt the butter. Beat in the superfine sugar, almond meal, flour, lemon zest and half the yoghurt.

Pour the dough onto cling wrap, then roll into a log and refrigerate overnight.

Preheat oven to 325°F (160°C).

Unwrap the dough and cut into rounds. Bake on baking paper for 15–20 minutes. Place on a wire rack to cool.

Combine confectioners' sugar with the remaining yoghurt and the lemon essence. Add enough water to make the confectioners' spreadable. Top each cookie with the icing.

Orange Crackles

preparation 50 mins **cooking** 17 mins
makes 26

4½oz (135g) unsalted butter, at
  room temperature

1¼ cups sugar

zest of 2 oranges

2 large egg yolks, at room
  temperature

1 teaspoon orange extract

2 cups all-purpose (plain) flour

¼ teaspoon baking soda
  (bicarbonate soda)

¼ teaspoon salt

1 cup confectioners' (icing) sugar,
  sifted

2 drops orange food colouring

2–3 tablespoons freshly squeezed
  orange juice

Preheat oven to 350°F (180°C).

Line 2 baking sheets with baking paper.

Beat the butter in a medium bowl with an electric mixer until smooth. Add the sugar and half the zest and continue to beat until light and fluffy, about 3 minutes. Add the egg yolks, 1 at a time, beating well after each addition. Beat in the orange extract

Sift the flour, baking soda and salt into a bowl, then gently stir into the butter mixture.

Drop heaped tablespoonfuls of the dough onto the baking sheets, leaving about 2in (5cm) between each. Freeze for 30 minutes.

Bake the cookies, straight from the freezer, until edges are firm and bottoms are lightly browned, about 15–17 minutes. Transfer to a rack and allow to cool completely.

Mix the confectioners' sugar, food colouring and remaining zest in a medium bowl. Add the orange juice and mix. Dip the top of the cookies into the icing, and leave to set for 45 minutes.

Lime and Bergamot Cookies

preparation 30 mins **cooking** 17 mins
makes 24

4½oz (135g) unsalted butter, at
  room temperature

1¼ cups sugar

zest of 1 lemon

zest of 1 lime

1 large egg, plus 1 yolk,
  at room temperature

¼ teaspoon lime essence

¼ teaspoon orange essence

3 drops bergamot oil

2 cups all-purpose (plain) flour

¼ teaspoon baking soda
  (bicarbonate soda)

¼ teaspoon salt

Preheat oven to 375°F (190°C).

Line 2 baking sheets with baking paper.

Beat the butter in a medium bowl with an electric mixer until smooth. Add the sugar and zests and continue to beat until light and fluffy, about 3 minutes. Add the egg and yolk one at a time, beating well after each addition. Beat in the essences and bergamot oil.

Sift the flour, baking soda and salt together in a bowl. Gently stir the dry ingredients into the butter mixture.

Drop heaped tablespoonfuls of the dough onto the baking sheets, leaving about 2in (5cm) between each. Place in refrigerator for 15 minutes.

Bake the cookies, straight from the refrigerator, until edges are firm and bottoms are lightly browned, about 15–17 minutes. Transfer to a rack to cool.

fruit & nut

Sultana Muesli Cookies

preparation 15 mins   **cooking** 10 mins
makes 26

4oz (125g) butter

2 tablespoons golden syrup

1 teaspoon baking soda
(bicarbonate soda)

½ cup sugar

½ cup unsweetened natural
muesli

½ cup sultanas

1 cup wholemeal flour

Preheat oven to 350°F (180°C). Lightly butter 2 oven trays.

Melt butter and golden syrup in a saucepan large enough to mix all the ingredients. Cool.

Dissolve baking soda in 1 tablespoon hot water. Add to saucepan with sugar, muesli, sultanas and flour. Mix well.

Place tablespoonfuls of mixture on the oven trays, leaving room to spread. Press lightly with a fork.

Bake for 10 minutes or until golden. Leave on the tray for 2 minutes, then place on a wire rack to cool.

Almond Cookies

preparation 10 mins **cooking** 15 mins
makes 24

3½oz (100g) butter

¼ cup golden syrup

½ teaspoon almond extract

½ cup sugar

1 cup rolled oats

½ cup desiccated coconut

½ cup all-purpose (plain) flour

½ cup almond meal

½ teaspoon baking soda
  (bicarbonate soda)

Preheat oven to 350°F (180°C). Line an oven tray with baking paper.

Melt the butter in a large saucepan. Add the golden syrup and stir to combine. Add the almond extract, sugar, rolled oats, coconut, flour and almond meal, then stir well.

Mix the baking soda with 2 tablespoons warm water. Add to the mixture and stir to combine. Roll the mixture into small balls and place on the baking paper. Flatten slightly, then bake for 12–15 minutes.

Toffee Almond Cookies

preparation 15 mins   **cooking** 10 mins
makes 30

6oz (180g) unsalted butter, at
 room temperature

3½oz (100g) brown sugar

1 egg

1 teaspoon almond extract

1 cup all-purpose (plain) flour

½ teaspoon salt

½ teaspoon baking soda
 (bicarbonate soda)

½ cup rolled oats

½ cup almond meal (flour)

½ cup almonds, chopped

1 cup toffee baking bits, chopped

Preheat oven to 300°F (150°C). Line 2 oven trays
with baking paper.

Cream together the butter and sugar until well
combined and pale in colour, fold through the
egg and almond extract. Sift the flour, salt and
baking soda into the mixture, then stir in the rolled
oats, almond meal, chopped almonds and toffee
pieces.

Drop heaped tablespoonfuls onto the baking
paper. Flatten slightly, then bake for 8–10 minutes.
Cool on the trays.

Peanut and Rye Cookies

preparation 10 mins   **cooking** 15 mins
makes 30

4oz (125g) butter

½ cup brown sugar

1 egg

¾ cup all-purpose (plain) flour

¾ cup rye flour

2 tablespoons cocoa powder

1½ teaspoons baking powder

¾ cup chopped peanuts

Preheat oven to 375°F (190°C). Lightly butter 2 baking trays.

Place butter and brown sugar in a saucepan large enough to mix all the ingredients. Heat until butter melts, then allow to cool. Add egg and beat in with a wooden spoon.

Sift flours, cocoa and baking powder into saucepan, then add the husks left in sifter to the saucepan and mix well. Add ½ cup of peanuts and stir until mixed through.

Place teaspoonfuls of mixture on the baking trays. Sprinkle with remaining nuts, flatten slightly and bake for 15 minutes or until cooked.

Blueberry Soft-bake Cookies

preparation 10 mins **cooking** 20 mins
makes 8

5oz (150g) all-purpose (plain) flour

1½ teaspoons baking powder

½ teaspoon ground cinnamon

2oz (55g) butter, cubed

3oz (85g) sugar

5 tablespoons milk

5oz (150g) fresh blueberries

Preheat the oven to 375°F (190°C). Lightly butter a large baking sheet.

Sift the flour, baking powder and cinnamon into a bowl. Rub in the butter, using your fingers, until the mixture resembles rough breadcrumbs, then stir in the sugar.

Stir in the milk and blueberries until just combined – the dough should be quite sticky.

Spoon 8 mounds, spaced well apart, onto the baking sheet and cook for 20 minutes or until golden and springy to the touch. Cool on a wire rack for a few minutes before serving.

NOTE These cookies are best eaten hot with a large scoop of ice cream.

Peanut Butter Cookies

preparation 40 mins **cooking** 15 mins
makes 24

7oz (200g) all-purpose
  (plain) flour

½ teaspoon baking powder

1 teaspoon ground cinnamon

4oz (125g) superfine (caster)
  sugar

4oz (125g) butter

1 egg, lightly beaten

½ cup raspberry jam

12 glacé cherries, halved

PEANUT BUTTER FROSTING

2 tablespoons butter

6 tablespoons smooth
  peanut butter

1 cup confectioners' (icing) sugar

Preheat oven to 350°F (180°C).

Sift flour, baking powder and cinnamon together, add sugar, then rub in butter with your fingers. Mix to a firm paste with the egg (if necessary, add a very little milk), then refrigerate for 30 minutes.

Roll out thinly, cut into small rounds with a cookie cutter, and bake until firm, about 15 minutes.

Meanwhile combine all the frosting ingredients with 2 tablespoons hot water and beat with a fork until well combined.

Remove cookies from oven and cool on a wire rack. Sandwich two biscuits together with a teaspoon of jam, put a little frosting on top and place a cherry half in the centre. Repeat with remaining cookies.

Banana, Oat and Nut Cookies

preparation 20 mins   **cooking** 15 mins
makes 20

9oz (250g) unsalted butter,
at room temperature

7oz (200g) brown sugar

7oz (200g) white sugar

2 eggs

1⅔ cups all-purpose (plain) flour

1 teaspoon baking soda
   (bicarbonate soda)

½ teaspoon salt

3 cups rolled oats

1 cup pecans, chopped

1 cup almonds, chopped

½ banana, mashed

Preheat oven to 375°F (190°C). Line 2 cookie sheets with baking paper.

Cream together the butter and sugars until well combined and pale in colour, add the eggs and fold through. Add flour, baking soda and salt. Once ingredients are thoroughly combined, add the oats, nuts and banana.

Drop tablespoonfuls onto the cookie sheets, about 1½in (10cm) apart. Flatten slightly, then bake for 10–15 minutes. Cool on a wire rack.

Cherry Delights

preparation 15 mins   **cooking** 15 mins
makes 40

4oz (125g) butter

1 tablespoon sugar

1 tablespoon golden syrup

6oz (170g) all-purpose (plain)
  flour

1 level teaspoon baking powder

few drops of vanilla extract

2oz (60g) glacé cherries, chopped

Preheat oven to 350°F (180°C). Line 2 oven trays
with baking paper.

Melt the butter, sugar and golden syrup together
in a saucepan. Sift the flour with the baking
powder.

Pour the melted mixture, while hot, into the
dry ingredients and mix quickly. Add vanilla and
cherry pieces and form into small balls.

Place on baking trays, leaving a gap between
them. Flatten slightly with a fork, then bake for
12–15 minutes. Remove and cool on a wire rack.

coffee

Cappuccino Chocolate Chip Cookies

preparation 20 mins   **cooking** 10 mins
makes 25

2 teaspoons instant coffee

1 tablespoon coffee liqueur

1 cup brown sugar

½ cup white sugar

6oz (180g) butter,
  at room temperature

1oz (30g) chocolate pieces,
  melted and cooled

2 eggs

1 teaspoon vanilla extract

2⅔ cups all-purpose (plain) flour

1 teaspoon baking powder

½ teaspoon ground cinnamon

2 cups chocolate chips

2½oz (75g) white chocolate

1 teaspoon vegetable oil

Preheat oven to 350°F (180°C). Line 2 baking sheets with baking paper.

Dissolve instant coffee in coffee liqueur in a small bowl.

Combine brown sugar, white sugar and butter in a large bowl. Beat at medium speed, scraping bowl often, until well mixed. Add coffee mixture, cooled melted chocolate, eggs and vanilla, continue beating until well mixed. Reduce speed to low, add flour, baking powder and cinnamon. Beat until well mixed. Stir in chocolate chips.

Drop teaspoonfuls of dough, 2in (5cm) apart, onto cookie sheets. Bake for 8–10 minutes or until golden brown. Allow to cool completely before decorating.

Place the white chocolate and oil in the microwave and cook for 20 second intervals until melted, stirring well between each 20 seconds. Do not overcook. Drizzle over cooled cookies.

Chewy Coffee Cookies

preparation 20 mins   **cooking** 14 mins
makes 25

4oz (125g) butter, at room
   temperature

½ cup brown sugar

1 large egg, plus 1 yolk

2 tablespoons coffee liqueur

⅓ cup molasses

3 tablespoons instant coffee

2½ cups all-purpose (plain) flour

1 teaspoon ground cinnamon

½ teaspoon ground cardamom

2 teaspoons baking soda
   (bicarbonate soda)

½ cup confectioners' (icing) sugar

Preheat oven to 350°F (180°C). Lightly butter 2
cookie sheets.

Cream the butter and brown sugar. Add egg,
egg yolk, liqueur and molasses, and fold together
thoroughly.

Combine instant coffee, flour, spices and baking
soda in a medium bowl. Add dry ingredients to
wet and work them in.

Roll mixture into balls, 2 tablespoonfuls at a time,
then roll the balls in the confectioners' sugar.
Place on the cookie sheets and bake for 12–14
minutes.

Coffee Snaps

preparation 20 mins   **cooking** 10 mins
makes 34

2oz (60g) butter

⅓ cup brown sugar, firmly packed

½ cup white sugar

1 egg

1½ teaspoons vanilla extract

1 tablespoon milk

2 cups all-purpose (plain) flour

½ teaspoon salt

¼ teaspoon baking soda
  (bicarbonate soda)

¼ teaspoon baking powder

2 tablespoons instant coffee

Preheat oven to 400°F (200°C). Line baking sheets with baking paper.

Beat the butter, brown sugar, white sugar, egg, vanilla and milk until smooth.

Combine the flour, salt, baking soda, baking powder and instant coffee. Add to sugar mixture and mix thoroughly.

Roll tablespoonfuls of dough into balls – if it's too soft, refrigerate until stiff enough. Place balls 1½in (4cm) apart on baking sheets. Flatten with a fork.

Bake for 8–10 minutes until lightly browned.

Coffee Sugar Cookies

preparation 1 hr 15 mins   **cooking** 8 mins
makes 24

4oz (120g) butter, at room temperature

¾ cup sugar

1 teaspoon baking powder

2 teaspoons instant coffee

1 egg

1 teaspoon vanilla extract

2 cups all-purpose (plain) flour

¼ cup confectioners' (icing) sugar

Preheat oven to 340°F (170°C).

Beat butter with an electric mixer. Add sugar, baking powder and coffee. Beat until well combined.

Beat in egg and vanilla, then half of the flour. With a wooden spoon, stir in the remaining flour. Cover and chill for 1 hour.

Divide the dough in half and roll each half out until ½in (1cm) thick. Cut into 2in (5cm) squares, make a mark down the centre, and place onto cookie sheets.

Bake for 8 minutes, until edges are firm and bottoms are lightly browned. Dust with confectioners' sugar.

Coffeetines

preparation 15 mins   **cooking** 10 mins
makes 24

½ cup single (thickened) cream

½ cup superfine (caster) sugar

1 cup hazelnuts, finely chopped

3½oz (100g) candied orange peel,
   finely chopped

2 teaspoons instant coffee

¼ cup all purpose (plain) flour

7oz (200g) chocolate

¼ teaspoon vegetable oil

2 tablespoons strong
   espresso coffee

Preheat oven to 340°F (170°C).

Mix together the cream, sugar, nuts, peel, instant coffee and flour to form a dough.

Drop 1 teaspoonful at a time onto baking paper, approximately 1¾in (4cm) apart. Flatten with a knife dipped in cold water.

Bake for 10 minutes, or until browned around the edges. Cool, flat side up, on racks.

Once completely cool, combine the chocolate, oil and espresso in a bowl and microwave until chocolate only just begins to melt, stirring every 20 seconds – be careful not to burn the chocolate. Spread chocolate over the flat side of each biscuit.

Super Espresso Cookies

preparation 15 mins   **cooking** 10 mins
makes 100

8½oz (240g) unsalted butter, at
  room temperature

1 cup brown sugar, firmly packed

1 cup white sugar

2 eggs

2 teaspoons vanilla extract

2¾ cups all-purpose (plain) flour

2 tablespoons instant coffee

1 teaspoon baking soda
  (bicarbonate soda)

½ teaspoon salt

9½oz (275g) chocolate covered
  coffee beans

1 cup pecans, roasted and
  chopped

Preheat oven to 350°F (180°C). Lightly butter
4 baking trays.

In an electric mixer, beat butter until smooth, add
sugars and mix well. Add the eggs, one at a time,
then add the vanilla extract.

Combine the flour, coffee, baking soda and salt
in a separate bowl. Slowly add the dry ingredients
to the butter mixture, and beat until thoroughly
mixed.

Stir in the chocolate-covered coffee beans and
pecans.

Drop half-tablespoonfuls onto baking trays. Bake
for 8–10 minutes. Allow to cool on the baking tray
for 2–3 minutes, remove to a wire rack to cool
completely.

Buzz Bites

preparation 20 mins **cooking** 12 mins
makes 70

½ cup extra virgin olive oil

⅔ cup raw sugar

2 tablespoons instant coffee

1 egg

¾ cup all-purpose (plain) flour

½ teaspoon vanilla extract

1 teaspoon malt powder

¼ cup Brazil nuts, chopped

¼ cup almonds, chopped

Preheat oven to 350°F (175°C). Lightly butter 3 cookie sheets.

In a medium bowl, cream together the oil, sugar and coffee. Beat in the egg, flour, vanilla, malt and nuts. Mix until well blended.

Drop teaspoonfuls onto the cookie sheets. Bake for 10–12 minutes or until edges are golden. Cool on wire racks.

Pecan Coffee Drizzles

preparation 30 mins **cooking** 10 mins
makes 20

5 teaspoons instant coffee

3½oz (100g) unsalted butter, at
   room temperature

3½oz (100g) brown sugar

1 egg, lightly beaten

10½oz (300g) all-purpose
   (plain) flour

1 teaspoon baking powder

2¾oz (75g) pecans, roughly
   chopped

2½oz (80g) milk chocolate, melted

2 tablespoons confectioners'
   (icing) sugar

Dissolve 4 teaspoons of the coffee in 1 tablespoon
boiling water. Set aside to cool slightly.

Beat together the butter and sugar in a bowl until
light and creamy, add the egg and beat well. Add
the flour, baking powder and coffee mixture, then
work together with your hands until the dough is
smooth. Refrigerate for 10 minutes.

Preheat oven to 350°F (180°C). Lightly butter a
baking tray.

Roll out half of the mixture between two sheets
of baking paper – the dough should be about ¼in
(5mm) thick. Cut into rounds using a 2½in (6cm)
cookie cutter. Repeat with the remaining dough.

Place the cookies on the baking tray and bake
for 10 minutes. Remove the cookies to a wire
rack and sprinkle with nuts

Melt the chocolate with the remaining coffee and
the confectioners' sugar and stir to combine.
Drizzle the melted chocolate mixture over the
cooled cookies. Leave to set.

Cinnamon Almond Cookies

preparation 20 mins **cooking** 8 mins
makes 18

1½oz (45g) butter, at room
   temperature

½ cup sugar, plus 2 tablespoons

4 tablespoons Amaretto

1 egg

2 cups flour

1½ tablespoons instant coffee

2 teaspoons ground cinnamon

Preheat oven to 375°F (190°C).

Cream the butter and ½ cup of the sugar in a large bowl until light and fluffy. Add the Amaretto and egg and mix well.

In a small bowl, whisk together the flour, coffee and 1 teaspoon of the cinnamon. Slowly mix the flour mixture into the butter mixture until thoroughly combined.

In a small bowl, combine the 2 tablespoons sugar and the remaining cinnamon. Shape tablespoonfuls of the dough into balls and roll in the sugar mixture. Place the balls 1½in (4cm) apart on a cookie sheet and flatten slightly with the palm of your hand.

Bake for 6–8 minutes. Immediately transfer to a wire rack to cool.

chocolate

Chocolate Ripple Cookies

preparation 15 mins   **cooking** 12 mins
makes 10

3½oz (100g) butter

3½oz (100g) milk chocolate,
  chopped

3 tablespoons cocoa powder

½ cup superfine (caster) sugar

1 teaspoon vanilla extract

1 egg, lightly beaten

1½ cups self-rising (self raising)
  flour, sifted

Preheat oven to 350°F (180°C). Line a baking tray with baking paper.

Place butter, chocolate and cocoa in a small saucepan over low heat. Cook, stirring, for 2 minutes or until chocolate has melted. Remove to a bowl and allow to cool for 5 minutes.

Add sugar, vanilla and egg to mixture. Mix well, then add flour. Stir until just combined.

Roll mixture into balls, 2 tablespoonfuls at a time. Place onto the baking tray and flatten slightly. Bake for 12 minutes or until firm to the touch. Cool for 5 minutes on the tray before transferring to a wire rack.

Chocolate Sour Cream Cookies

preparation 20 mins **cooking** 17 mins
makes 40

6oz (180g) unsalted butter, at
　room temperature

1 cup light brown sugar

½ cup white sugar

2 eggs, at room temperature

1 teaspoon vanilla extract

⅓ cup sour cream

2⅔ cups all-purpose (plain) flour

1 teaspoon baking soda
　(bicarbonate soda)

1 teaspoon salt

2 cups semi-sweet chocolate chips

1 cup macadamias,
　crushed

Preheat oven to 350°F (180°C). Line 2 oven trays
with baking paper.

In a large bowl, cream butter and sugars until
fluffy. Add eggs and vanilla and mix thoroughly.
Add sour cream and combine well.

In a medium bowl, combine flour, baking soda
and salt. Slowly add to the butter mixture and mix
until well combined. Gently fold in chocolate and
nuts.

Drop teaspoonfuls of dough 1½in (4cm) apart on
the baking paper. Bake for 15–17 minutes or until
golden brown and the middle is soft to the touch.
Cool on a wire rack.

Crunchy Choc Cookies

preparation 10 mins   **cooking** 10 mins
makes 30

1 cup crunchy peanut butter

7oz (200g) butter, at room
temperature

1 tablespoon vanilla extract

1 egg, lightly beaten

7oz (200g) brown sugar

1 cup all-purpose (plain) flour

1 teaspoon baking soda
   (bicarbonate soda)

1 cup milk chocolate chips

1½ cups pecans, coarsely
chopped

Preheat oven to 400°F (200°C). Line 2 cookie
sheets with baking paper.

Combine peanut butter, butter, vanilla and egg
in a bowl, then add the sugar, flour and baking
soda. Mix thoroughly, then fold through chocolate
and pecans.

Roll heaped tablespoonfuls into balls and place
on the cookie sheets. Press lightly with the back
of a fork and bake for 8–10 minutes. Cool on the
cookie sheets.

Chocky Road Cookies

preparation 20 mins   **cooking** 10 mins
makes 36

6oz (180g) butter, at room
   temperature

1 cup brown sugar

2 eggs, lightly beaten

2½ cups all-purpose (plain) flour

½ cup cocoa powder

½ cup buttermilk

6½oz (185g) white chocolate,
   roughly chopped

1 cup dry-roasted peanuts

1 cup chocolate chips

Preheat oven to 350°F (180°C). Lightly butter
2 baking trays.

Place the butter and sugar in a bowl and beat
until light and fluffy. Gradually beat in the eggs.

Sift together the flour and cocoa powder. Add
the flour mixture, buttermilk, white chocolate,
peanuts and chocolate chips to the egg mixture
and combine well.

Drop tablespoonfuls onto the baking trays and
bake for 10 minutes or until cooked. Transfer to
wire racks to cool.

Chocolate Brown Cookies

preparation 10 mins   **cooking** 20 mins
makes 12

1oz (30g) unsalted butter, melted

¼ cup cocoa powder

1 cup sugar

2 large eggs

pinch of salt

1 cup all-purpose (plain) flour,
   sifted

1 teaspoon baking powder

Preheat oven to 350°F (180°C). Line an oven tray with baking paper.

Combine the butter, cocoa, sugar, eggs and salt in a bowl. Add the flour and baking powder and stir well.

Place 12 spoonfuls of mixture on the baking paper. Bake for 15–20 minutes.

Fudge Chocolate Cookies

preparation 20 mins **cooking** 10 mins
makes 24

4oz (125g) butter, chopped

1 teaspoon vanilla extract

1¼ cups brown sugar, firmly
    packed

1 egg

1 cup all-purpose (plain) flour

¼ cup self-rising (self-raising)
    flour

1 teaspoon baking soda
    (bicarbonate soda)

⅓ cup cocoa powder

½ cup raisins

¾ cup macadamias, toasted and
    coarsely chopped

½ cup dark chocolate chips

½ cup dark chocolate melts,
    halved

Preheat oven to 350°F (180°C). Line 2 oven trays
with baking paper.

Beat butter, vanilla, sugar and egg in a medium
bowl with an electric mixer until smooth.

Sift the flours together with the baking soda and
cocoa powder, then stir into the butter mixture
with the raisins, nuts and chocolate.

Drop rounded tablespoonfuls of mixture onto the
trays about 1½in (4cm) apart, press each with a
fork to flatten slightly. Bake for 10 minutes.

Stand the cookies for 5 minutes, then transfer to
a wire rack to cool.

Chocolate Peanut Cookies

preparation 20 mins   **cooking** 15 mins
makes 25

¾ cup all-purpose (plain) flour

¼ teaspoon baking powder

½ teaspoon salt

4oz (125g) unsalted butter, at
  room temperature

¾ cup brown sugar

2 tablespoons superfine (caster)
  sugar

1 vanilla pod, split in half
  lengthwise

1 egg

3 teaspoons milk

1 cup rolled oats

1 cup unsalted peanuts

1 heaped cup dark chocolate chips

Preheat oven to 325°F (160°C). Line 2 baking
trays with baking paper.

Combine flour, baking powder and salt in a bowl.

Beat the butter, brown sugar, superfine sugar and
seeds from vanilla pod in an electric mixer until
the mixture has become thick and pale.

Add the egg and milk, then beat in the flour
mixture with the rolled oats. Fold in the peanuts
and chocolate.

Drop tablespoonfuls of the dough onto the
baking trays. Bake for 15 minutes, then remove
from the oven and allow to cool on a wire rack.

Malto Bites

preparation 20 mins   **cooking** 15 mins
makes 15

6oz (175g) unsalted butter, at
  room temperature

3 tablespoons superfine (caster)
  sugar

1 cup all-purpose (plain) flour

2 tablespoons malt powder

½ teaspoon vanilla extract

3½oz (100g) dark chocolate,
  roughly chopped

1 cup hazelnuts, ground

Preheat oven to 340°F (170°C).

Cream butter and sugar well. Fold the flour into butter mixture with the malt and vanilla, then add the chocolate and nuts and combine.

Roll into balls and flatten slightly with a fork. Bake for 15 minutes.

Double Troubles

preparation 15 mins   **cooking** 12 mins
makes 20

⅓ cup extra light olive oil

3½oz (100g) milk chocolate, chopped

½ cup superfine (caster) sugar

1 teaspoon vanilla extract

1 egg, lightly beaten

1½ cups self-rising (self raising) flour, sifted

½ cup hazelnut spread

1¾oz (50g) dark chocolate chips

Preheat oven to 350°F (180°C). Line a baking tray with baking paper.

Place oil and milk chocolate into a small saucepan over low heat. Cook, stirring with a metal spoon, for 2 minutes or until chocolate has melted. Remove to a bowl. Allow to cool for 5 minutes.

Add sugar, vanilla and egg. Mix well. Add flour and stir with a wooden spoon until just combined.

Roll mixture into balls, 2 teaspoonfuls at a time. Place onto the baking tray and flatten slightly.

Use the end of a wooden spoon to make an indentation in the centre of each biscuit. Fill each indentation with ½ teaspoon of hazelnut spread, then place dark chocolate chips on top. Place tray in freezer for 15 minutes or until biscuits are firm.

Bake biscuits for 12 minutes or until firm to the touch. Cool for 5 minutes on the tray before transferring to a wire rack.

Chocomarsh Cookies

preparation 30 mins **cooking** 12 mins
makes 12

2oz (60g) butter, at room
   temperature

½ cup brown sugar, firmly packed

1 egg

2 teaspoons vanilla extract

1½ cups all-purpose (plain) flour,
   sifted

½ cup superfine (caster) sugar

¾ tablespoon gelatine powder

5oz (150g) dark chocolate, melted

¼ cup confectioners' (icing) sugar

Preheat oven to 325°F (160°C). Line a baking tray with baking paper.

Cream butter and brown sugar in a large bowl until smooth. Add egg and 1 teaspoon of vanilla and mix well. Fold in flour.

Place mixture on a lightly floured surface and roll out to ¼in (5mm) thickness. Cut out circles with a 2½in (6cm) round biscuit cutter and place on the baking tray.

Bake for 10–12 minutes or until golden and cooked. Cool on trays.

Meanwhile, combine superfine sugar and ½ cup water in a small saucepan, then sprinkle in gelatine powder. Stir over low heat until sugar and gelatine dissolve. Bring to the boil, then reduce heat and simmer for 4 minutes. Remove and cool.

When almost cold, pour mixture into a bowl, add remaining vanilla and beat with an electric mixer for 3–4 minutes until very thick.

Spoon marshmallow mixture into a piping bag fitted with a plain ½in (1cm) nozzle and pipe onto half the biscuits. Top with remaining biscuits, pressing gently. Place biscuits in refrigerator for about 15 minutes until marshmallow is firm. Remove from fridge, spread with melted chocolate and dust with icing sugar.

Hazelchocs

preparation 20 mins **cooking** 20 mins
makes 16

4oz (120g) butter

4 tablespoons superfine (caster)
sugar

4 tablespoons brown sugar

1 cup all-purpose (plain) flour

3 tablespoons rice flour

2 tablespoons cornstarch
(cornflour)

2 tablespoons instant coffee, plus
1 teaspoon

2 tablespoons milk

3 tablespoons hazelnuts, toasted
and finely chopped

½ cup chocolate hazelnut spread

3½oz (100g) dark cooking
chocolate, melted

Preheat oven to 340°F (170°C). Lightly butter 2
baking trays.

Beat butter and sugars in a small bowl with an
electric mixer until pale and fluffy. Stir in sifted
flours and 2 tablespoons of the coffee in two
batches, then stir in milk and nuts.

Roll tablespoonfuls into balls and flatten slightly.
Place 1¼in (3cm) apart on the baking trays. Bake
for about 20 minutes or until pale golden. Cool on
a wire rack.

Meanwhile, combine hazelnut spread and
chocolate in a bowl. Refrigerate, stirring often,
until spreadable.

Join 2 biscuits with 1–2 teaspoons of hazelnut
chocolate. Repeat with remaining biscuits.

biscotti

Choc-almond Biscotti

preparation 15 mins   **cooking** 1 hr 20 mins, plus 15 mins cooling
makes 35

2 cups all-purpose (plain) flour

⅓ cup cocoa powder

1 teaspoon baking soda
(bicarbonate soda)

1¾oz (50g) butter, melted

2 tablespoons milk

2 tablespoons dark rum

1 cup sugar

7oz (200g) blanched almonds

2 eggs, plus 1 egg yolk

Preheat oven to 340°F (170°C). Lightly butter a baking tray.

Sift the flour, cocoa powder and baking soda into a bowl. Mix in the butter, milk and rum. Make a well in the centre of the flour mixture, add the sugar, almonds and eggs and mix well to form a soft dough.

Turn the dough onto a lightly floured surface and knead until smooth. Divide the dough in half, and form each half into a log 1½in (4cm) high and 1½in (4cm) wide. Place on the baking tray, brush with egg yolk, then bake for 30 minutes.

Remove from oven and allow to cool for 15 minutes. Turn oven down to 285°F (140°C).

Using a serrated knife, cut logs into ½in (1½cm) slices and return to baking tray. Bake for another 50 minutes until crisp.

Biscotti Classico

preparation 15 mins   **cooking** 1 hr 20 mins, plus 15 mins cooling
makes 25

10oz (280g) all-purpose (plain)
  flour

1 teaspoon baking powder

1 teaspoon salt

1 cup superfine (caster) sugar

zest of 2 lemons

1 tablespoon instant coffee

2 teaspoons aniseed powder

3oz (85g) unsalted butter

5oz (150g) hazelnut meal

2 eggs

5 tablespoons Galliano

Preheat oven to 340°F (170°C). Lightly butter a baking tray.

Sieve flour, baking powder and salt into a large bowl. Add sugar, zest, coffee and aniseed.
Rub in the butter until the mixture resembles breadcrumbs. Stir through the hazelnut meal.

Whisk the eggs with the Galliano and add to the other ingredients. Mix until a dough forms, and gently knead to bind all the ingredients.

Divide in half, and form each half into a log 1½in (4cm) high and 1½in (4cm) wide. Place on the baking tray, then bake until golden brown, about 30 minutes.

Remove from oven and allow to cool for 15 minutes. Turn oven down to 285°F (140°C).

Using a serrated knife, cut logs into ½in (1½cm) slices and return to baking tray. Bake for another 50 minutes until crisp.

Pecan Choc Biscotti

preparation 15 mins   **cooking** 1 hr 20 mins, plus 15 mins cooling
makes 25

10oz (280g) all-purpose (plain) flour

3oz (85g) cocoa powder

1 teaspoon baking soda (bicarbonate soda)

1 teaspoon salt

1 cup superfine (caster) sugar

3oz (85g) unsalted butter

3½oz (100g) pecans, ground, plus 1¾oz (50g) roughly chopped

5oz (150g) chocolate chips

3 eggs

2½ tablespoons chocolate liqueur

Preheat oven to 340°F (170°C). Lightly butter a baking tray.

Sieve flour, cocoa, baking soda and salt into large bowl, add the sugar. Rub in the butter until the mixture resembles breadcrumbs. Stir through the ground pecans, chopped pecans and chocolate chips.

Whisk the eggs with the chocolate liqueur and add to the other ingredients. Mix until a dough forms, and gently knead to bind all the ingredients.

Divide in half, and form each half into a log 1½in (4cm) high and 1½in (4cm) wide. Place on the baking tray, then bake for 30 minutes.

Remove from oven and allow to cool for 15 minutes. Turn oven down to 285°F (140°C).

Using a serrated knife, cut logs into ½in (1½cm) slices and return to baking tray. Bake for another 50 minutes until crisp.

Coffee Biscotti Fingers

preparation 15 mins   **cooking** 5 mins
makes 32

3 eggs, separated

5oz (140g) superfine (caster)
  sugar

⅓ cup all-purpose (plain) flour

1¼oz (35g) potato flour

1 tablespoon instant coffee

1 vanilla pod, split in half
  lengthwise

Preheat oven to 350°F (180°C). Lightly butter
sponge finger trays.

Whisk egg yolks and sugar until pale and creamy.

Beat the egg whites until they are quite firm, fold
into yolk mixture.

Sift both flours into the egg mix, add coffee and
seeds from vanilla pod, and fold through gently.

Place heaped teaspoons in the moulds, sprinkle
with extra superfine sugar, and cook for 5 minutes.

Orange Biscotti

preparation 15 mins   **cooking** 1 hr 20 mins, plus 15 mins cooling
makes 25

10½oz (300g) all-purpose (plain) flour

1 teaspoon baking powder

1 cup superfine (caster) sugar

zest of 2 oranges

1 teaspoon instant coffee

½ teaspoon aniseed powder

3oz (85g) butter

5oz (150g) almond meal

2 eggs

4 tablespoons Grande Marnier

Preheat oven to 340°F (170°C). Lightly butter a baking tray.

Sieve flour and baking powder into a large bowl. Add the sugar, zest, instant coffee and aniseed. Rub in the butter until the mixture resembles breadcrumbs. Stir through the almond meal.

Whisk the eggs with the Grande Marnier and add to the other ingredients. Mix until a dough forms, and gently knead to bind all the ingredients.

Divide in half, and form each half into a log 1½oz (4cm) high and 1½oz (4cm) wide. Place on the baking tray, then bake until golden brown, about 30 minutes.

Remove from oven and allow to cool for 15 minutes. Turn oven down to 285°F (140°C).

Using a serrated knife, cut logs into ½in (1½cm) slices and return to baking tray. Bake for another 50 minutes until crisp.

Biscotti Brasiliani

preparation 15 mins   **cooking** 1 hr 20 mins, plus 15 mins cooling
makes 25

10oz (280g) all-purpose (plain) flour

3oz (85g) cocoa powder

1 teaspoon baking soda (bicarbonate soda)

1 cup superfine (caster) sugar

3oz (85g) butter

5oz (150g) Brazil nuts, roughly chopped

3½oz (100g) chocolate chips

3 large eggs

4 tablespoons rum

Preheat oven to 340°F (170°C). Lightly butter a baking tray.

Sieve flour, cocoa and baking soda into a large bowl, add the sugar. Rub in the butter until the mixture resembles breadcrumbs. Stir through the Brazil nuts and chocolate chips.

Whisk the eggs with the rum and add to the other ingredients. Mix until a dough forms, and gently knead to bind all the ingredients.

Divide in half, and form each half into a log 1½in (4cm) high and 1½in (4cm) wide. Place on the baking tray, then bake for 30 minutes.

Remove from oven and allow to cool for 15 minutes. Turn oven down to 285°F (140°C).

Using a serrated knife, cut logs into ½in (1½cm) slices and return to baking tray. Bake for another 50 minutes until crisp.

Choc-mint Biscotti

preparation 15 mins   **cooking** 1 hr 20 mins, plus 15 mins cooling
makes 35

14oz (400g) all-purpose (plain)
flour

1 tablespoon cocoa powder

1 teaspoon baking powder

1 cup superfine (caster) sugar

½ teaspoon salt

3oz (85g) unsalted butter

5oz (150g) hazelnut meal

5oz (150g) chocolate chips

3 eggs

5 tablespoons crème de menthe

Preheat oven to 340°F (170°C). Lightly butter a baking tray.

Sieve flour, cocoa and baking powder into a large bowl, add sugar and salt. Rub in the butter until the mixture resembles breadcrumbs. Stir through the hazelnut meal and chocolate chips.

Whisk the eggs with the crème de menthe and add to the other ingredients. Mix until a dough forms, and gently knead to bind all the ingredients.

Divide in half, and form each half into a log 1½in (4cm) high and 1½in (4cm) wide. Place on the baking tray, then bake until golden brown, about 30 minutes.

Remove from oven and allow to cool for 15 minutes. Turn oven down to 285°F (140°C).

Using a serrated knife, cut logs into ½in (1½cm) slices and return to baking tray. Bake for another 50 minutes until crisp.

Butterscotch Biscotti

preparation 15 mins **cooking** 1 hr 20 mins, plus 15 mins cooling
makes 25

10oz (280g) all-purpose (plain) flour

1 teaspoon baking powder

¼ teaspoon salt

1 cup superfine (caster) sugar

zest of 1 lemon

1 teaspoon malt powder

1 teaspoon aniseed powder

3oz (85g) unsalted butter

5oz (150g) hazelnut meal

3¾oz (110g) almond meal

2 eggs

5 tablespoons butterscotch schnapps

Preheat oven to 340°F (170°C). Lightly butter a baking tray.

Sieve flour, baking powder and salt into a large bowl. Add sugar, zest, malt and aniseed. Rub in the butter until the mixture resembles breadcrumbs. Stir through the hazelnut meal and almond meal.

Whisk the eggs with the butterscotch schnapps and add to the other ingredients. Mix until a dough forms, and gently knead to bind all the ingredients.

Divide in half, and form each half into a log 1½in (4cm) high and 1½in (4cm) wide. Place on the baking tray, then bake until golden brown, about 30 minutes.

Remove from oven and allow to cool for 15 minutes. Turn oven down to 285°F (140°C).

Using a serrated knife, cut logs into ½in (1½cm) slices and return to baking tray. Bake for another 50 minutes until crisp.

Biscotti Bianca Bocca

preparation 45 mins   **cooking** 1 hr 20 mins, plus 15 mins cooling
makes 25

1½oz (40g) dried white
mulberries, roughly chopped

2 tablespoons strawberry liqueur

10oz (280g) all-purpose (plain)
flour

1 cup superfine (caster) sugar

1 teaspoon baking powder

1 tablespoon malt powder

⅓ teaspoon aniseed powder

½ teaspoon salt

3oz (85g) unsalted butter

5oz (150g) hazelnut meal

2 eggs

2 tablespoons crème de cassis

Coat the mulberries in the strawberry liqueur and set aside for 30 minutes.

Preheat oven to 325°F (160°C). Lightly butter a baking tray.

Sieve flour into a large bowl, then add sugar, baking powder, malt, aniseed and salt. Rub in the butter until the mixture resembles breadcrumbs. Stir through the hazelnut meal and mulberries.

Whisk the eggs with the crème de cassis and add to the other ingredients. Mix until a dough forms, and gently knead to bind all the ingredients.

Divide in half, and form each half into a log 1½in (4cm) high and 1½in (4cm) wide. Place on the baking tray, then bake until golden brown, about 30 minutes.

Remove from oven and allow to cool for 15 minutes. Turn oven down to 285°F (140°C).

Using a serrated knife, cut logs into ½in (1½cm) slices and return to baking tray. Bake for another 50 minutes until crisp.

Biscotti Mandorle

preparation 15 mins   **cooking** 1 hr 20 mins, plus 15 mins cooling
makes 25

10½oz (300g) flour

1 cup superfine (caster) sugar

1 tablespoon aniseed powder

3oz (85g) butter

5oz (150g) almond meal

4oz (125g) blanched almonds

¼ cup pine nuts

2 eggs

4 tablespoons crème de cacao

Preheat oven to 340°F (170°C). Lightly butter a baking tray.

Sieve flour into a large bowl, add the superfine sugar and aniseed. Rub in the butter until the mixture resembles breadcrumbs.

Stir through the almond meal, blanched almonds and pine nuts.

Whisk the eggs with the crème de cacao and add to the other ingredients. Mix until a dough forms, and gently knead to bind all the ingredients.

Divide in half, and form each half into a log 1½in (4cm) high and 1½in (4cm) wide. Place on the baking tray, then bake until golden brown, about 30 minutes.

Remove from oven and allow to cool for 15 minutes. Turn oven down to 285°F (140°C).

Using a serrated knife, cut logs into ½in (1½cm) slices and return to baking tray. Bake for another 50 minutes until crisp.

wheat-free

Wheat-free Peanut Butter Cookies

preparation 20 mins **cooking** 12 mins
makes 18

4oz (125g) butter, at
   room temperature

6oz (175g) light brown sugar

6oz (175g) rice flour

1 teaspoon baking powder

1 large egg, beaten

4oz (125g) crunchy peanut butter

Preheat oven to 350°F (180°C). Lightly butter a baking tray.

Cream butter and sugar together, mix in the flour and baking powder. Stir through the egg and peanut butter.

Roll into balls and flatten slighty. Place on the baking tray and cook for 10–12 minutes.

Cherry Fig Dimples

preparation 20 mins   **cooking** 12 mins
makes 24

3½oz (100g) butter

1¾oz (50g) superfine (caster)
   sugar

9oz (250g) Lola's all-purpose flour
   (see below)

1 egg

1 tablespoon molasses

¼ cup cherry jam

12 dried baby figs, cut in half

LOLA'S ALL-PURPOSE FLOUR

14oz (400g) besan flour, also
   known as chickpea, gram,
   channa dahl or dahl flour

14oz (400g) maize cornflour

7oz (200g) potato flour, also
   known as potato starch (use the
   finest grind you can find)

7oz (200g) yellow maize flour,
   also known as stone-ground
   maize flour

Preheat oven to 350°F (180°C). Line an oven tray with baking paper.

Combine all ingredients except jam and figs in a food processor and process until combined.

Roll tablespoonfuls of dough into balls and press onto the tray using your thumb, leaving a small indentation.

Top each cookie with ½ teaspoon of jam, then with a piece of fig. Bake for 12 minutes, then cool on the tray.

Lola's All-Purpose Flour

Place the ingredients in a large plastic bag and give the bag a good shake.

Place a sieve or pasta strainer in a second plastic bag. Pour the flour into the strainer in the bag and shake to sift. The flour is now ready for use.

NOTE Store in a paper or calico bag so the flour can breathe (two tea towels stitched together with a string tie make a good flour bag that can be easily laundered). Stored this way, the flour will keep in good condition for several years. Do not keep this flour in an airtight container – a loose-lidded or flip-top container is suitable, as long as the flour can breathe.

Christmas Cookies

preparation 15 mins   **cooking** 10 mins
makes 24

¼ cup olive oil

2 tablespoons treacle

10½oz (300g) Lola's all-purpose
flour (see Cherry Fig Dimples)

½ cup superfine (caster) sugar

2 tablespoons ground ginger

1 tablespoon mixed spice

1 egg, lightly beaten

5oz (150g) white chocolate

Preheat oven to 300°F (150°C). Cover a tray with baking paper.

Place the oil and treacle in a saucepan and gently warm. Remove from the heat and add three-quarters of the flour and the remaining ingredients except the chocolate. Mix well with a wooden spoon.

Tip onto a plastic sheet or board and knead the remaining flour into the pastry. Roll out between two sheets of cling wrap. Cut out in desired shapes and place on the tray.

Place in the centre of the oven and bake for 10 minutes, until just firm to touch. Cool on the tray.

Meanwhile, melt chocolate in a bowl over simmering water. When the biscuits are cold, ice with chocolate.

Wheat-free Date Cookies

preparation 10 mins   **cooking** 25 mins
makes 16

2½oz (75g) butter

2½oz (75g) rice flour

½ teaspoon baking soda
   (bicarbonate soda)

1¾oz (50g) rolled oats

9oz (250g) fresh dates, chopped

3½oz (100g) mixed nuts, chopped

3½oz (100g) sultanas

1 teaspoon almond extract

2 eggs, beaten

Preheat oven to 325°F (160°C). Line an oven tray with baking paper.

Rub butter into flour. Sieve in the baking soda, stir in the oats, add the dates, nuts and sultanas. Stir in the almond extract and the eggs.

Roll the dough into balls, 2 tablespoonfuls at a time, and place on the oven tray. Flatten slightly, then bake for 25 minutes.

Ginger Fingers

preparation 1 hr   **cooking** 15 mins
makes 14

3½oz (100g) Lola's all-purpose
   flour (see Cherry Fig Dimples)

1 teaspoon ground cinnamon

3½oz (100g) sugar

1 teaspoon nutmeg

1 tablespoon ground ginger

¾oz (25g) baby rice cereal

1 teaspoon baking soda
   (bicarbonate soda)

¾oz (25g) desiccated coconut

4 tablespoons olive oil

3½oz (100g) treacle

Preheat the oven to 325°F (160°C). Line an oven tray with baking paper.

Place the dry ingredients into a mixing bowl and whisk to ensure they are evenly distributed.

Pour the oil, treacle and 1 tablespoon water into a large saucepan and bring to a boil. Remove the saucepan from the heat and add the dry ingredients, stirring well to combine.

Tip the mixture onto a sheet of cling wrap and press into a long bar shape. Refrigerate for 30 minutes.

Unroll the cling wrap and, using a knife that has been dipped in olive oil, cut the bar into thick strips. Lift onto the oven tray with a spatula and press lightly with a fork.

Cook for 10 15 minutes until a deep golden brown.

Currant and Coconut Crisps

preparation 25 mins   **cooking** 30 mins
makes 30

3 eggs

1½ cups superfine (caster) sugar

7oz (200g) Lola's all-purpose flour
(see Cherry Fig Dimples)

4oz (125g) currants

5oz (150g) desiccated coconut

2 teaspoons vanilla extract

Preheat oven to 325°F (160°C). Lightly butter 2 large oven trays or cover with baking paper.

Place the eggs and sugar in a large bowl and hand whisk over a saucepan of hot water until the mixture is lukewarm and frothy. Remove from the heat and continue beating with an electric beater until the mixture will hold its shape.

Combine the flour with the currants and coconut. Carefully fold the dry ingredients into the whipped egg mixture, then add the vanilla and mix.

Place teaspoonfuls of mixture onto the prepared trays in rough heaps, leaving plenty of room for the cookies to spread. Bake for 20 minutes.

Turn the heat off and leave the cookies in the oven for an additional 10 minutes.

Wheat-free Florentines

preparation 15 mins **cooking** 15 mins
makes 22

3½oz (100g) Lola's all-purpose
flour (see Cherry Fig Dimples)

3½oz (100g) sugar

1 teaspoon gluten-free baking
powder

¾oz (25g) baby rice cereal

1oz (30g) almond meal

1½oz (40g) flaked almonds

⅓ cup olive oil

2 tablespoons pear syrup
concentrate

3 teaspoons vanilla extract

3 teaspoons almond extract

3 tablespoons glucose

7oz (200g) chocolate, melted

Preheat the oven to 400°F (200°C). Line 2 oven
trays with baking paper.

Combine the dry ingredients in a large bowl and
mix to combine.

Place the oil, pear syrup, vanilla and almond
extracts, glucose and 1 tablespoon water in a
large saucepan and bring to the boil. When the
liquid is boiling and frothy, remove from the heat,
add the dry ingredients and stir well.

Place teaspoonfuls of the mixture onto the
baking paper in small mounds, leaving room for
the mixture to spread to about three times its
size.

Put the baking trays in the oven, reduce the heat
to 300°F (150°C) and bake the cookies for
5 minutes. Open the oven door and press the
cookies flat with a fork. Continue cooking for
an additional 10 minutes until they are golden
and quite flat. Flatten again if they rise too much
(they need to be flattened to make them crisp).
Remove from the oven and cool on the tray.

Coat one side with melted chocolate.

Shortbread Creams

preparation 10 mins **cooking** 20 mins
makes 12

4oz (125g) butter

9oz (250g) Lola's all-purpose flour
(see Cherry Fig Dimples)

1 egg

3½oz (100g) superfine (caster)
sugar

2 teaspoons vanilla extract

2 teaspoons raspberry jam

7oz (200g) pure confectioners'
(icing) sugar

Preheat oven to 325°F (160°C). Line an oven tray with baking paper.

Combine all ingredients except jam and confectioners' sugar in a food processor and process until combined.

Roll tablespoonfuls of dough into balls and press onto the tray with a fork. Bake for 20 minutes.

Heat the jam with 2 teaspoons water, sift in the confectioners' sugar and heat until dissolved.

Allow the cookies to cool completely, then sandwich two biscuits together with the raspberry icing. Repeat with remaining biscuits.

Choc-topped Cookies

preparation 20 mins   **cooking** 30 mins
makes 30

4 egg whites

5oz (150g) superfine (caster)
  sugar

3½oz (100g) brown sugar

2 teaspoons vanilla extract

3½oz (100g) Lola's all purpose
  flour (see Cherry Fig Dimples)

3½oz (100g) rice flour

5oz (150g) dark chocolate

Preheat the oven to 300°F (150°C). Cover 2 baking trays with baking paper.

Place the egg whites, superfine sugar, brown sugar and vanilla in a large bowl and hand whisk over a saucepan of hot water until the mixture is slightly warm and frothy. Remove from the heat and continue beating with an electric beater until the mixture is stiff. Fold in the combined flours.

Using a teaspoon or piping bag and large star pipe, mound the mixture in little peaks on the baking tray. Leave one cookie space between each peak for them to spread.

Bake for 20 minutes, then leave for a further 10 minutes with the oven door partly open. Cool on the tray.

Melt dark chocolate in a double boiler and dip the top of the cookies in the chocolate.

Almond wheat-free Cookies

preparation 20 mins   **cooking** 15 mins
makes 16

3½oz (100g) Lola's all-purpose
  flour (see Cherry Fig Dimples)

½ cup sugar

1 teaspoon baking soda
  (bicarbonate soda)

1½oz (40g) flaked almonds

¾oz (25g) ground almonds

¾oz (25g) baby rice cereal

4 tablespoons olive oil

3 tablespoons glucose

3 teaspoons vanilla extract

1 teaspoon almond extract

Preheat the oven to 325°F (160°C). Cover a baking tray with foil or baking paper.

Whisk the flour, sugar, baking soda, flaked almonds, ground almonds and rice cereal in a mixing bowl to combine.

Place the oil, glucose and 2 tablespoons of water in a large saucepan and heat slowly to a simmer. Remove the saucepan from the heat and add the dry ingredients. Add the vanilla and almond extracts and mix well.

Turn onto a sheet of cling wrap and roll into a long sausage shape. (At this stage the cookie dough can be left in the refrigerator until needed – if well wrapped, it will keep for a week. Remove from refrigerator and bring to room temperature before slconfectioners' to bake.)

Slice the dough into 16 portions using a sharp knife, and place on the baking tray.
Cook for about 10–15 minutes until a pale golden colour. Cool on the tray.

cookie
extras

Coconut and Lime
Ice Cream Sandwiches

preparation 15 mins
makes 4

½ cup superfine (caster) sugar

zest of 1 orange

2 tablespoons fresh orange juice, strained

4 scoops vanilla ice cream

8 Citrus Snaps (see recipe)

1 cup flaked coconut, toasted

zest of 4 limes

Combine the sugar and ½ cup of water in a small pan, stir over a low heat until the sugar is dissolved.

Bring the mixture to the boil, then add the orange zest and juice. Reduce the heat and simmer, uncovered, for 5 minutes. Remove from the heat and cool.

Place the ice cream on half of the biscuits, and top with remaining biscuits.

Sprinkle over the toasted coconut and the lime zest. Pour over the orange syrup and serve.

Chocolate Ripple Cake

preparation 15 mins, plus 24 hrs refrigeration
serves 4

1¼ cups single (thickened) cream

1 teaspoon superfine (caster) sugar

1 teaspoon vanilla extract

9oz (250g) Chocolate Ripple Cookies (see recipe)

Combine cream, sugar and vanilla and whip until very stiff.

Place a generous spread of cream on one biscuit, stand it on its side, then do the same with another biscuit and stand it next to the first. Continue with the remaining biscuits until you have made a log.

Cover the log entirely with the remaining cream. Place in refrigerator for at least 24 hours.

To serve, cut cake at an angle to ensure alternate layers of cookies and cream are in each slice.

Lemon Ginger Cake

preparation 30 mins, plus 24 hrs refrigeration   **cooking** 10 mins
serves 4

8 Gingerbread Men (see recipe)

1¼ cups cream

1 teaspoon superfine (caster)
sugar

½ teaspoon lemon essence

Make the gingerbread dough, but cut into round discs. Bake according to the recipe.

Combine cream, superfine sugar and lemon essence, and whip until very stiff.

When the biscuits have cooled, place a generous spread of lemon cream on one gingerbread disc, stand it on its side, then do the same with another gingerbread disc and stand it next to the first. Continue with the remaining gingerbread discs until you have made a log.

Cover the log entirely with the remaining cream. Place in the refrigerator for at least 24 hours.

To serve, cut cake at an angle to ensure alternate layers of cookies and cream are in each slice.

Caramel Malted Cake

preparation 15 mins, plus 24 hrs refrigeration
serves 4

1¼ cups single (thickened) cream

1 teaspoon superfine (caster) sugar

2 tablespoons caramel topping

1 teaspoon malt powder

8 Malto Bites (see recipe)

½ cup banana chips

Combine cream and sugar and whip until very stiff. Fold through the caramel topping.

Place a generous spread of caramel cream on one Malto Bite, stand it on its side, then do the same with another and stand it next to the first. Continue with the remaining Malto Bites until you have made a log.

Cover the log entirely with the remaining cream. Place in refrigerator for at least 24 hours. Before serving, decorate with banana chips.

To serve, cut cake at an angle to ensure alternate layers of cookies and cream are in each slice.

Streusel Rum Cake

preparation 15 mins   **cooking** 45 mins
serves 10

¾ cup sugar

1½oz (45g) unsalted butter, at
 room temperature, plus 3oz
 (90g) melted

1 egg

½ cup milk

1¾ cups all-purpose (plain) flour

2 teaspoons baking powder

¼ teaspoon salt

6 Ginger Fingers (see recipe)

½ cup rum

1 cup brown sugar

2 teaspoons ground cinnamon

1 cup walnuts, chopped

¼ cup confectioners' (icing) sugar

Preheat oven to 350°F (180°C). Lightly butter a
7¾ x 7¾in (20 x 20cm) tin.

Beat together the sugar, 1½oz (45g) of the butter
and the egg. Stir in the milk. Sift together 1½ cups
of the flour, the baking powder and salt, then blend
into the butter mixture.

Spread of the mixture in the tin. One by one,
crumble the biscuits evenly into the tin, then
sprinkle with rum. Top with the remaining cake
mixture.

Mix together the brown sugar, remaining flour,
cinnamon, melted butter and walnuts, and
sprinkle evenly over the cake.

Bake for 40–45 minutes or until a skewer pushed
in the centre comes out clean.

Dust with confectioners' sugar

Chocolate Cookie Pudding

preparation 15 mins   **cooking** 55 mins
serves 4

4 day-old Double Troubles (see
   recipe), crumbled

½ cup sugar

⅓ cup unsweetened cocoa powder

¼ teaspoon ground cinnamon

¼ teaspoon salt

2 eggs

2 cups milk

½ teaspoon vanilla extract

1 tablespoon vegetable oil

Preheat oven to 350°F (180°C).

Lightly butter a 7¾ x 7¾in (20 x 20cm) baking dish. Cover the bottom of the baking dish with an even layer of the crumbled biscuits.

In a small bowl, mix the sugar, cocoa, cinnamon and salt.

In a medium bowl, whisk together the eggs, milk, vanilla and vegetable oil. Add the sugar mixture and stir until combined.

Pour evenly over the biscuits. Press down with the back of a large spoon.

Place the baking dish into a larger, high sided baking dish. Pour boiling water halfway up the sides of the outside dish. Bake for 55 minutes, or until set.

Cookies and Cream Semi-freddo

preparation 10 mins, plus 6 hrs refrigeration
serves 4

3 egg yolks

1 can condensed milk

4 teaspoons vanilla extract

1 cup Chocolate Ripple Cookies
(see recipe), crushed

2 cups single (thickened) cream,
whipped

In a large bowl, beat the egg yolks, then stir in the condensed milk and vanilla. Fold in the cookies and cream.

Pour mixture into a 9 x 4¾in (23 x 12cm) loaf tin lined with foil. Cover and freeze for 6 hours or until firm.

To serve, scoop from tin or cut into slices.

Hedgehog

PREPARATION 10 mins, plus 1hr 20 mins refrigeration
makes 12 slices

6oz (175g) butter

⅔ cup superfine (caster) sugar

4 tablespoons cocoa powder

2 tablespoons desiccated coconut

1 egg, lightly beaten

½ cup shelled pistachios, roughly
  chopped

9oz (250g) Traditional Shortbread
  (see recipe), broken into pieces

9oz (250g) dark cooking
  chocolate, coarsely chopped

¼ cup confectioners' (icing) sugar

In a saucepan, melt 4oz (125g) of the butter, the sugar and cocoa over a medium heat for 3 minutes, stirring to dissolve sugar. Remove from heat and add coconut, egg, pistachios and shortbread.

Line a 28 x 18cm baking tin with baking paper, then press the mixture into the tin. Chill for 1 hour.

Melt chocolate and remaining butter in a bowl over simmering water. Spread over slice. Refrigerate for 20 minutes, then dust with confectioners' sugar and cut into pieces with a hot knife.

New York-style Cheesecake

preparation 15 mins, plus 4 hrs refrigeration   **cooking** 45 mins
makes 12 slices

1¼ cups Lemon Short Stars (see recipe), crushed

¼ cup sugar

2½oz (80g) butter, melted

1½ cups sour cream

1 cup sugar

2 eggs

zest of 1 lemon

17½oz (500g) cream cheese, broken into small pieces

Preheat oven to 330°F (165°C).

Blend the biscuit crumbs, sugar and half the melted butter, then line the bottom of a 9in (23cm) springform tin.

Blend the sour cream, sugar, eggs and lemon zest in a food processor for 1 minute. Add the cream cheese, blend until smooth. While blending, pour the remaining butter through the top of the machine. Pour cream cheese mixture into the springform tin.

Bake in the lower third of the oven for 45 minutes, remove from oven and cool.

Refrigerate for at least 4 hours, preferably overnight. Dust with plenty of confectioners' sugar before cutting and serving. Serve with whipped cream.

Peach Crumble Cake

preparation 20 mins **cooking** 60 mins
makes 12 slices

6oz (175g) unsalted butter, at room temperature, plus ¾oz (25g) finely chopped

¾ cup superfine (caster) sugar

3 eggs, lightly beaten

1½ cups self-rising (self-raising) flour

1 teaspoon baking powder

1 cup almond meal

14oz (400g) canned peach slices

2 tablespoons all-purpose (plain) flour

3½oz (100g) Citrus Snaps (see recipe), roughly chopped

¼ cup brown sugar, firmly packed

Preheat oven to 350°F (180°C). Lightly butter a round, 8½in (22cm) cake tin. Line with non-stick baking paper.

Beat 6oz (175g) of the butter and the superfine sugar together in an electric mixer until pale and creamy. Add the eggs, one at a time, beating well after each addition. Stir in the self-rising flour, baking powder and almond meal.

Spoon cake mixture into the cake tin and smooth the surface. Arrange the peaches over the top of the cake, pressing down gently.

Combine the all purpose flour, citrus snaps, brown sugar and the chopped butter in a small bowl. Sprinkle over the peaches.

Bake for 50–60 minutes or until a skewer inserted into the centre comes out clean. Remove from oven. Set aside for 15 minutes before turning onto a wire rack to cool.

Serve with yoghurt.

Tiramisu

preparation 25 mins, plus 2 hrs refrigeration
serves 8

1 vanilla pod

2 eggs, separated

½ cup superfine (caster) sugar

9oz (250g) cream cheese

9oz (250g) mascarpone

1 cup strong black coffee, cooled

¼ cup coffee liquour

22 Coffee Biscotti Fingers (see
   recipe)

1¾oz (50g) milk chocolate, grated

Cut the vanilla pod in half and scrape out the seeds.

Combine the egg yolks, sugar and cream cheese in a mixing bowl. Beat together with an electric beater until light. Add the mascarpone and vanilla seeds and stir to combine.

In a separate bowl, beat the egg whites until soft peaks form. Fold the egg whites into the cream cheese mixture.

Mix the coffee and liqueur together in shallow dish. Dip each biscuit in the coffee mixture.

Place half the biscuits in a 12 x 8in (30 x 20cm) dish. Spoon over half the cream mixture, top with the remaining biscuits and then the remaining cream mixture.

Garnish with grated chocolate. Cover and place in the refrigerator for 2 hours or overnight.

Index